IT'S PUB TIME, ANDY CAPP

by Smythe

A FAWCETT GOLD MEDAL BOOK

Fawcett Publications, Inc., Greenwich, Conn.

CLICK

BLIMEY, THE STUFF THEY'RE PUTTIN' ON — 'ERE I AM PLAYIN' TRUANT FROM ME 'OUSEWORK TO WATCH THE SAME FILM I PLAYED TRUANT FROM SCHOOL TO SEE!

I'VE BEEN TOTTIN' UP, YOU SPEND AS MUCH ON BOOZE AS YOU ALLOW ME F' HOUSEKEEPIN'!

YER WORTH IT, SWEET'EART, EVEN IF I AM OVERPAYIN' YER

Smythe

2-15-71

REMEMBER, NOW, DON'T 'AVE TOO MANY — I KNOW WHAT YER LIKE WHEN YER GET THE TASTE

GRR! GRR!

MAN'S ALREADY NINETY PER CENT WATER, AN' STILL YER NOT SATISFIED!

Smythe 2-18-71

I'M OFF, PET—

NO INTEREST, THAT'S YOU! YER MIGHT AT LEAST SAY *WATCH YER STEP* OR *KEEP OUT OF BAD COMPANY!*

2-22-71

I'VE NEVER 'AD A MOMENT'S WORRY —CAN YOU IMAGINE 'IM MEETIN' ANYBODY WORSE THAN 'IMSELF?!

Smythe

Smythe

BLIMEY, YER'VE GOT IMAGINATION, I'LL SAY THAT F'YER!

WHAT ARE YER ON ABOUT?

4-14-71

WHY DID YER TELL THAT WOMAN IT WAS ME DANCIN' THAT FIRST ATTRACTED YER? — I CAN'T DANCE A STEP

I 'AD TO THINK OF SOME EXCUSE

THANK YOU! THANK YOU VERY MUCH!

Smythe

DON'T THINK I DIDN'T SEE YER! I WALK MILES AN' MILES LOOKIN' F' YER, AN' F' WHAT? - THE SHOCK OF FINDIN' YER WITH HER!

WHY IS IT THAT PEOPLE WHO GET SHOCKED SO EASY GO OUT OF THEIR WAY TO FIND THINGS THAT WILL?

IT'S TEEMIN' DOWN! WHAT A DAY FOR A GIRL TO 'AVE TO GO OUT TO WORK!

5.7.71

EVERYBODY MOANS ABOUT THE WEATHER BUT NOBODY DOES ANYTHIN' ABOUT IT, EH, PET? HEH! HEH! HEH!

YOU DO, MATEY — YER STAY INDOORS!

OOO! SHE CAN 'AVE A VERY NASTY TONGUE IN THE MORNIN'S

Smythe

LOOK AT ME — EXHAUSTED! 'OW Y' CAN LET A WOMAN OF MY AGE GO OUT T' WORK, I DO NOT KNOW!

5-20-71

PET, WHEN WE MET — DIDN'T I PROMISE T' KEEP YOU IN THE MANNER TO WHICH YOU WERE ACCUSTOMED?

YOU DID

AN' WHEN WE MET, WERE YER WORKIN'?

I WAS

THEN SHADDUP!!

Smythe

OH, BLIMEY, LOOK AT THAT CLOCK—!

6-5-71

FLO—?

COMING—

PHEW!

—BOP—

SHE 'AD ME WORRIED THERE FOR A WHILE —A BLOKE'S *REALLY* PAST IT WHEN 'IS MISSUS DOESN'T CARE WHAT TIME 'E COMES IN!

Smythe

7-5-71

DON'T GET THE IDEA THAT I'M A DOG, BECAUSE I'M NOT—!

I'M A BARMAID WHO'S ALLOWED TO SIT DOWN OCCASIONALLY

Smythe

7-15-71